Big Cats

Cheetahs

by Marie Brandle

Bullfrog

Ideas for Parents and Teachers

Bullfrog Books let children practice reading informational text at the earliest reading levels. Repetition, familiar words, and photo labels support early readers.

Before Reading

- Discuss the cover photo. What does it tell them?

- Look at the picture glossary together. Read and discuss the words.

Read the Book

- "Walk" through the book and look at the photos. Let the child ask questions. Point out the photo labels.

- Read the book to the child, or have him or her read independently.

After Reading

- Prompt the child to think more. Ask: What did you know about cheetahs before reading this book? What more would you like to learn about them?

Bullfrog Books are published by Jump!
5357 Penn Avenue South
Minneapolis, MN 55419
www.jumplibrary.com

Library of Congress Cataloging-in-Publication Data

Names: Brandle, Marie, 1989– author.
Title: Cheetahs / Marie Brandle.
Description: Minneapolis, MN: Jump!, Inc., [2021]
Series: Big cats | Includes index.
Audience: Ages 5–8 | Audience: Grades K–1
Identifiers: LCCN 2020022613 (print)
LCCN 2020022614 (ebook)
ISBN 9781645277170 (hardcover)
ISBN 9781645277187 (ebook)
Subjects: LCSH: Cheetah—Juvenile literature.
Classification: LCC QL737.C23 B7243 2021 (print)
LCC QL737.C23 (ebook) | DDC 599.75/9—dc23
LC record available at https://lccn.loc.gov/2020022613
LC ebook record available at https://lccn.loc.gov/2020022614

Editor: Eliza Leahy
Designer: Michelle Sonnek

Photo Credits: Eric Isselee/Shutterstock, cover, 1, 3, 11, 16, 23tl, 23br, 24; Shutterstock, 4; Roger de la Harpe/Shutterstock, 5; Carl Dupont/Shutterstock, 6–7, 23bl; Mark Bridger/Shutterstock, 8–9, 23tm; WLDavies/iStock, 10; Dr Ajay Kumar Singh/Shutterstock, 12–13, 23bm; WorldFoto/Alamy, 14–15; Chris HarveyPanth/SuperStock, 17; JS Sudan/Shutterstock, 18–19; GUDKOV ANDREY/Shutterstock, 20–21, 23tr.

Printed in the United States of America at Corporate Graphics in North Mankato, Minnesota.

Table of Contents

Super Speed

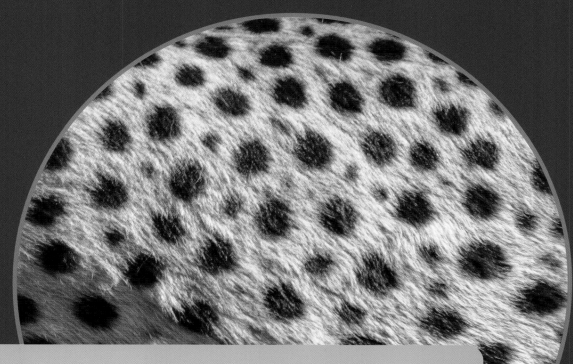

What big cats have yellow fur with black spots?

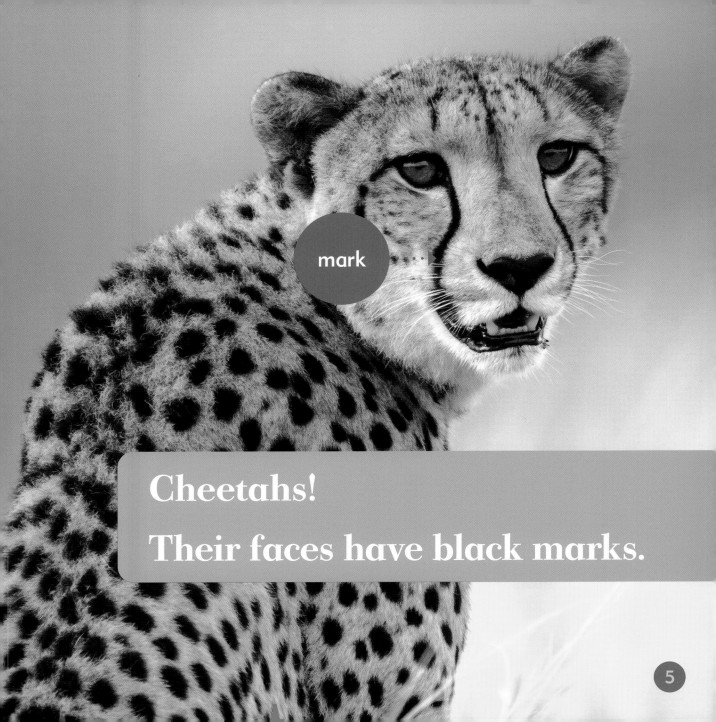

mark

Cheetahs!

Their faces have black marks.

5

Some live in grasslands.

Where?

Most live in Africa.

grassland

7

Their fur helps
them hide.

It blends in with
the grass.

They can see far.
This one sees prey.

She is quiet.

She stalks it.

wildebeest

Then she runs!
What does she hunt?
A wildebeest!

13

The cheetah is the fastest land animal.

Count to three.

In that time, a cheetah runs as fast as a car!

Wow!

See her long tail?

It helps her balance.

tail

16

See her sharp claws?
They grip the ground.

claw

17

The prey gets away.
The cheetah rests.
She drinks water.

She goes back to her cubs.

They will grow up.

They will hunt, too!

cub

Where in the World?

Most cheetahs live in grasslands in Africa. Some also live in savannahs, deserts, or mountains. A small number live in Asia. Take a look!

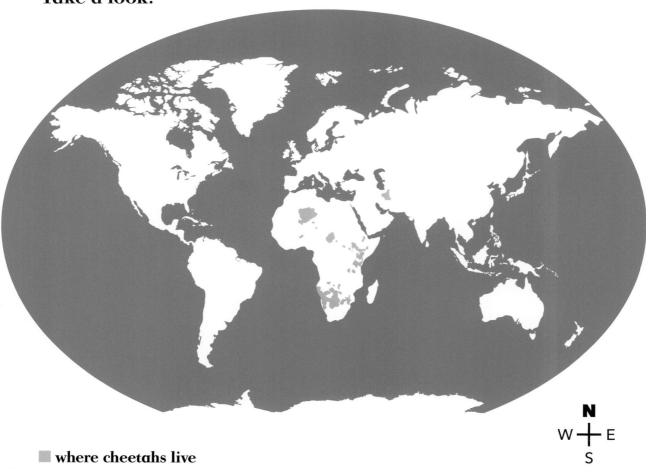

■ where cheetahs live

Picture Glossary

balance
To keep steady.

blends
Mixes in with another so that the two things combine together.

cubs
Young cheetahs.

grasslands
Large, open areas of grass.

prey
An animal that is hunted by another animal for food.

stalks
Hunts or tracks an animal in a quiet, secret way.

Index

To Learn More

Finding more information is as easy as 1, 2, 3.

❶ Go to www.factsurfer.com

❷ Enter "cheetahs" into the search box.

❸ Choose your book to see a list of websites.